Why Are We Here? Workbook

7 Building Blocks
and
7 Exercises
for
Understanding and Applying
the Ultimate Truths about Life

by

Dennis Marcellino

A Companion Workbook for *Why Are We Here?*

Why Are We Here? Workbook

Printed in the United States of America

Published By
Lighthouse Publishing
PO Box 40
Gladstone, OR 97027
e-mail: LighthouseOrders@aol.com
e-mail: Dennis@UltimateTruths.com

www.UltimateTruths.com

ISBN-13: 978-0-945272-12-0
ISBN-10: 0-945272-12-X

Table of Contents

This workbook will take you on a very exciting investigation into the ultimate questions of life (in my opinion, the most exciting).

The book, *Why Are We Here?*, has in-depth scientific evidence about the ultimate questions of life. This workbook doesn't repeat the same information but is put together as a way to help you apply what you read in that book and to give you some additional information.

Take a moment to really think about the following questions:

Does God exist?

The science of logic says there can be only one answer to this question. **Either God exists or doesn't exist.**

And if God does exist, who is this God who exists? What can we know about him (her or it). *Note:* We will be using the pronoun "he" to describe God for simplicity sake.

So how do we know if God exists, especially since he is obviously invisible to our eyes?

And what about the Bible or other religious books, how do we know if they are true or accurate and how true?

Let's start our examination with looking at some ideas about God. There are a lot of ideas and religions in the world that we could tap into and accept in regards to this question of God's existence.

Name a few ideas about God's existence and characteristics from various societies and religions:

____

____

____

____

____

____

____

____

____

____

And nearly all people in the world do accept one of those ideas as an explanation of the mystery behind the seemingly infinite universe and the fact that we just appeared here on this planet and will be forced to leave at one point. Those things are just too compelling and fascinating to ignore. So we have to attach to some explanation.

Also, people want to know what is going to happen (if anything) after they die.

Will they continue on in some way?

And will that way be reincarnation or purgatory or heaven or hell or nothing?

Will they see their loved ones again?

And does what we do with our lives now have on any influence on what our fate will be after we die?

So because of the potential of that last question, what we determine to be the truth about the universe, the birth/life/death reality and the afterlife has a very important impact on how we live the very real lives we have now.

Therefore, determining what is true about the universe and the afterlife is a critical requirement of this life now.

To Conclude: It is very much to our advantage to know the truth about the universe and the afterlife. In fact it is critical. Otherwise, how we live our life is a very risky gamble in terms of what will happen afterward, especially in light of what you'll be reading in *Why Are We Here?* and this workbook.

One last thought:

> **"Behind faith there must be truth or faith is**
> **merely superstition or empty ritual.**
> **Behind hope there must be truth or hope**
> **is merely wish or false confidence.**
> **Behind love there must be truth or**
> **you have mere emotion, sentiment,**
> **lust, or mutual deception."**
> – *Rev. Michael Maslowsky*

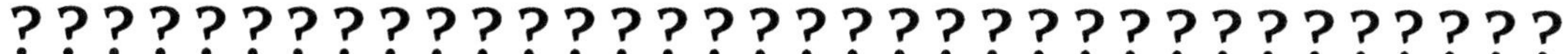

So, can we know what is true?

?????????????????????????????????????

How would we go about determining what is true?

I mean, there are so many concepts about deity that have floated around in human history and that still float around now. But they can't all be true because one of them (the God of the Bible) says that he is the ONLY God. Therefore, the God of the Bible and all of the other conceptions of God can't all be true simultaneously or co-exist (at least not as deity or God.)

If the God of the Bible is the only true God, there is even the possibility that the other gods people have worshiped throughout history could be "evil spirits" presenting themselves as gods because the Bible says that at least one evil spirit, satan, seeks to and actually does rule over people and nations.

But worshipping evil spirits in the place of God has led to evil and horrific things... like the Aztecs sacrificing 20% of their children and pulling their hearts out beating before they die. Their god, was called the "stone serpent" (sounds remarkably like the "serpent" villain in the Garden of Eden.)

But of course, half of a million Aztecs were conquered by just a few hundred Christian conquistadors led by Cortez, which seems like a military "miracle".

So we could even speculate that the real God stepped in and ended the barbaric behavior of the Aztecs through a military miracle, and then converted them to Christianity through another miracle at Guadalupe, which we'll investigate later.

But that's getting off the track a little. Let's go back to our investigation of "if" there is a God, then who is that God, and how can we be sure that He or She or It exists.

One thing which is not a proof God exists but is interesting to note is that:

Nearly all people believe there is a God.

A recent USA Today/CNN/Gallup polls say that 97% of Americans believe that God exists. In fact, Aldous Huxley, in *The Perennial Philosophy*, said that all groupings of people throughout all of the ages have had 3 things in common (as was expressed in their artifacts [totem poles, cave drawings, etc.] and by their group spokespersons/philosophers [witch doctors, priests, etc]. And these groups include cavemen, Africans, Asians, Europeans, New Guinea tribes, etc., many of whom never had physical contact or communication with any other group).

The 3 things in common found in all societies and human groupings throughout history are:

(1) They all believed in an invisible intelligence and world beyond the physical one.

(2) They believed that this invisible intelligence is a part of every human being, and

(3) The purpose of life is to discover God.

But that 97% figure drops way down when it comes to this question: **How many people know and understand the specifics about a real God and implement those specifics in their life?**

So, back to our investigation as to how we can know those things

Being that most people "believe" that God exists, the questions become: which specific belief are we talking about... and how did they come to that belief? Does God exist and what things are true about God?

Is their belief Muslim or Jewish or New Age or Protestant or Catholic or pagan or science or indigenous or mainstream myth, etc.?

I mean, we all have a story as to whose story we came to believe (or reject) and how and why we came to believe (or reject) it.

Now we'll take time to take a close look at your beliefs.

Exercise #1

Before continuing on, stop and write down your answers to the following questions (and give full and specific details in your answers):

1. Do you believe God exists?

2. If so, why... if not, why not?

3. Did you get your belief from another person or organization? If so, who?

4. WHY did you accept their belief (or whichever way you came to believe)?

5. What specifically do you believe is true *about* God?

___

___

___

___

___

___

___

___

___

___

Continuing with our investigation...

I'm going to show you how I personally came to my conclusions about God and the Bible. Because I needed to have scientific proof and no logical dead ends, you'll see how I satisfied those needs.

I started out as a person who was just focused on having fun... even if that meant engaging in what the church that I grew up in called sin.

In fact as a teenager, I completely abandoned my religious upbringing for the titillations of the world.

Being that I'm ambitious, that eventually led to me becoming a member of some of the most famous music groups in the world at that time: Sly & The Family Stone, The Elvin Bishop Group, The Electric Flag, Rubicon, and The Tokens (the band famous for their hit "The Lion Sleeps Tonight").

But that approach eventually brought a lot of pain, tragedies, failed relationships, intensely painful drug and alcohol experiences, and a specific emptiness inside that made me see my life of fun as shallow and unreal.

Being that I didn't like or want the painful experiences, I started investigating how I could not have to experience them. That investigation started with psychology.

I mean the mainstream thinking was: if you have a problem, you go to the doctor. If you have a life or experiential problem, you go to the doctor that deals with those kinds of problems. Since I had discounted religion (probably because I, and the peer group that I identified with, saw it as being too restrictive) that meant that I would go to a psychologist or psychiatrist.

To make a long story short (which I explain fully in my book *Why Are We Here?*, plus on a chart called "The Journey Of My Search For Truth", which you can see at my website: www.UltimateTruths.com), nothing I got involved in was able to resolve my dilemmas of:

(1) how to live this life without stepping into pain-causing errors, and...

(2) how to know *the* truth about this existence in a way that was completely satisfying intellectually and experientially.

I went through *many* psychology, new age, personal growth and lifestyle approaches, but none of them were able to satisfy those two dilemmas in such a way that worked. And by "worked" I mean gave me ways to think and live that produced strength and peace in my heart, and harmony in my life, and gave me an explanation of the truth about life that my mind (which was trained as an engineer) couldn't find a problem or logical violation with.

As you know, because of what is said on the back cover of my book, I finally did find both of those things in Christianity. So now with this workbook, I'm going to show you how you can also find that same sureness in your mind, and peace, joy and strength in your heart.

Clues about the Invisible in the Visible

First let's start investigating what we can know about the invisible by what we can see in the visible.

☐ Building Block #1

What Jesus and the Bible say, prove to be the most intellectually sound and effective ways to live when applied to individual lives.

People who apply what the Bible teaches experience good "fruit" in their lives that they didn't have before, including inner peace. I found this to be true in my life after having had *many* experiences and studies and methods that I submitted to (as I described earlier)... none of which worked.

Not until I actually became a Christian and submitted my life and actions to God's ways (as expressed in the Bible especially the New Testament) did the *power* come into my heart to be peaceful, secure and deeply fulfilled.

That power, which is promised to Christians in the Bible, also gave me the ability to not follow my sinful inclinations and impulses, a power that I previously did not have.

So a conclusion here is that if the Bible is true, then if a person doesn't have that kind of power, they really aren't fully practicing what the Bible teaches. That's one reason why I try to spread the Bible teachings... even to Christians; many of whom I can see don't fully realize the immense potential that is in Christianity.

Remember, Jesus said that if we even have the faith that a mustard seed has, we could move mountains. So if we can't move a mountain, that means that there is room for us all to grow in our faith.

Matt. 13:31-32: *"He proposed another parable to them. 'The kingdom of heaven is like a mustard seed that a person took and sowed in a field. It is the smallest of all the seeds, yet when full-grown it is the largest of plants. It becomes a large bush, and the birds of the sky come and dwell in its branches.' "*

Building Block #2

Being that we have to choose a personal approach to life, I found (after my MANY experiences, involvements and studies) that the greatest choice possible in the world to pattern my life after is the Bible. But that means every word in the Bible and a correct overall and specific understanding of what they mean.

Exercise #2

Write down your personal approach to life. Be as detailed as you can.

____

____

____

____

____

____

____

____

____

Building Block #3

Being that we are creatures with needs outside of ourselves, and being that those things require involvement with other people, we have to align with something more than ourselves. The most advanced system on earth is in the Bible.

> "The moral and religious system which Jesus Christ transmitted to us is the best the world has ever seen, or can see."
>
> – *Benjamin Franklin*

Exercise #3

Write down how and why you need other people and systems in the world.

Exercise #4

Write down the errors that you see happening with those people and systems.

So now we've just looked at two *very real* ways *in real life* that require us to deal with what we believe is true and is the best way to approach life. So in this sense we've moved out of the invisible and into the visible.

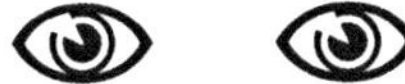

But let's continue along those lines.

Let's start with a logical question.

I determined that Jesus had spoken the most profound, effective and clear descriptions of and solutions for life (based on my studies, experience and training in psychology and sociology). But how could I know that the rest of what he said was true... things that were seemingly unprovable by me?

For example, he said that he was God. How could I prove or disprove that? He said that he was going to prepare a place for his followers in a place called Heaven. How could I know if that was true?

He said that the gate to Heaven was narrow, and that even many of those who called him "Lord" and said they did many great works in his name would not be going to Heaven. How could I know if that was true?

Well... Jesus said that if we won't believe him by his words, we should then believe him because of his works. I already

had come to see that his work in terms of his words of wisdom, psychological and sociological solutions were the best by applying them to my own life and they worked when nothing else worked.

For example, when I forgave people who sinned against me, instead of feeling bitter, I felt better, and then it made sense, because I also have sinned against others and wanted to be forgiven. Plus, when people sin they might (as Jesus said) "know not what they do." There is an "ultimate" scenario here.

(But of course, affinity for the other can't be restored unless there is also repentance...an apology.) Now, that approach worked better than any other approach I had encountered in the world. And there are *many* other examples, like: it is better to give than receive. When I gave myself to serving others, instead of feeling drained, I was rewarded in my heart with the most pleasurable of all feelings: **peace and love.**

When you actually try that one on you see that when you give (in a holy way), a giving happens to *you* in your heart in that pleasurable experiences like love and joy just appear there. And then that starts to make sense in your mind when you come to understand God's whole system, which is exemplified by the top person, Jesus, washing the feet of those who are below him and even allowing himself to experience a torturous death on a cross for their benefit.

(This also answers the question "why are we here?" which can be seen in chapter 4 of my book by the same title. The answer is: to learn and transform to this ultimate, perfect

system for how free will beings can peacefully, lovingly and harmoniously co-exist).

Here are some examples of other words and concepts in the Bible (which I was just being introduced to) that immediately resolved problems that I had been having.

 **"God hates sin."** ***(Psalms 45:8)***

That elevated me out of a pollyannaish "peace and love only" hippie approach and reunited me with a strong, emotional, internal desire (which had always been there but was suppressed) for there to be order in life that is based on a harmony with the true design of humans as physical, mental, emotional, social and spiritual beings. And this suppression also took away other parts of my true, natural, spontaneous being.

"It is better to dwell in a corner of the housetop than in a roomy house with a quarrelsome woman." ***(Proverbs 21:9)***

That freed me from wasting my time and stress in an unreal expectation that the quarrelsome woman that I lived with would ever come around to being nice, loving and reasonable.

"Have no anxiety at all, but in everything, by prayer and petition, with thanksgiving, make your requests known to God. Then the peace of God that surpasses all understanding will guard your hearts and minds in Christ Jesus." ***(Philippians 4:6,7)***

That gave me a simple formula for how to approach life that freed me from ever feeling anxiety. And, unlike many psychology approaches I tried, (including years of weekly therapy sessions), this one actually worked in that my feelings also went along with the plan for the first time. It gave me a whistle-while-you-work peace as I lived out a life based on inspiration (as opposed to obedience to others that went against my deepest feelings).

And I was quickly introduced to another verse to back that approach up:

"Render unto Caesar what is Caesar's and to render unto God what is God's." ***(Matthew 22:21)***

That meant that I didn't have to go against how God was inspiring me anymore.

Overall, I was thrilled... because for the first time, it all was working. I was directly now experiencing the great results of another Bible verse:

"Know the truth, and the truth will set you free." ***(John 8:32)***

That's one big reason why I came to strongly feel that with the Bible I had hit upon the truth. I was seeing proof... very positive changes within my own being, a being that I had worked on for years and had come to know well.

I hope to encourage you to do the same kind of experimenting with applying the Bible's precepts to your life and thereby receiving the same confidence in the Bible like I did.

I had worked hard for 14 years on trying to make those positive changes happen naturally within my being, through trying 22 different lifestyles and philosophies, included most of the popular forms of: psychology, new age, secular humanistic approaches, Scientology and religion... but without result... until I tried the Bible.

Just knowing that there was this new (to me) great system and world (Kingdom of God) that I was moving into freed me from many toxic attachments that I had not been able to let go of (which I clung to and tried to make work because I didn't know there was anything better. That is one reason why I work hard to tell people about God and the Bible... so that they'll know that there is something better).

I was also convinced by the "words" of Jesus and the rest of the Bible from a deductive reasoning viewpoint.

After years of investigating, thinking, studying, analyzing and scrutinizing the Bible and applying its precepts, I realized that there is no other possible explanation that can stand up to scientific and logical scrutiny... (and I spent over 20 years after coming to the Bible being open to seeing if there were irreconcilable flaws because I wanted to know if it really was all true. Even though I thought that I saw flaws on occasion, they always turned out to be reconcilable.

That brings in another proof from the mathematical discipline of "Probability and Statistics". That is, if there are no errors in such a large body of knowledge and facts as the Bible in what can be proven to be true, that gives what can't be proven or disproven a 100% probability of being all true).

☐ Building Block #4

Jesus and the Bible are the greatest source of psychological and sociological solutions in human history.

Now being that Jesus had that much credibility with me because he said the greatest statements and offered the greatest solutions in my main study, psychology... why would I assume that he was lying in the rest of the things that he said... especially when he spoke out so heavily against lying?

So then it would be more logical for me to assume that he wasn't lying about the other things he said, including the statements a few paragraphs back and him saying that he ***is*** God (in John 8:58).

After an extensive and objective search that spanned many years, I found the pinnacle on this planet in two of my main focuses (psychology and sociology) in Jesus and the Bible, but for some who have different focuses, that might not be proof enough.

So let's look at other proofs regarding Jesus.

✍ **The fact that Jesus performed miracles ("works") was confirmed by many non-Christian historians of His day (e.g. Jewish historian Josephus, Roman historians Cornelius Tacitus, Suetonius, Pliny the Younger, and Syrian Mara bar Serapion).**

But we must also consider the writers of the Bible to be credible historians, who even were eyewitnesses to His resurrection and had a number of encounters with Jesus during the 40 days after His resurrection until His Ascension while He was in His resurrected body that had supernatural powers. The credibility of the apostles is especially powerful given a quote in my book by current Supreme Court Justice Antonin Scalia. He had a humorous way of pointing out how absurd it is to conclude that the apostles didn't really witness the resurrection like they said they did.

Scalia said, "We must pray for the courage to endure the scorn of 'the sophisticated world'. The 'wise' do not believe in the resurrection of the dead. It is really quite absurd [to them]. The Ascension had to be made up by groveling enthusiasts as part of their plan to get themselves martyred".

The inference obviously is: why would most of the Apostles, especially the ones who were intelligent enough to write Scripture that has withstood the test of intense scrutiny for almost 2000 years, allow themselves to be killed (and mostly in horrible ways) for something that they knew wasn't

true? Perhaps one could be speculated to be crazy, but not 12 (with the 12th being Paul). And like I said, these writers also attested to seeing Jesus perform many other miracles that had the power to overcome natural laws, which no human on their own could do. And they themselves were even given supernatural powers so as to prove the credibility of their words (which is how Jesus also proved the credibility of his words).

☐ Building Block #5

Therefore, it is not logical or historical to think that Jesus' miracles and resurrection didn't occur. There is no other logical explanation that stands up to intense scrutiny.

☐ Building Block #6

We don't have to just rely on historical evidence that miracles existed. There are scientifically proven modern day miracles... Miracles exist and have been proven by scientists and can be verified by our senses and scientific instruments in the present.

The only scientific proof of the supernatural (i.e. instances where the laws of nature have been overcome) are all tied to Christianity. Even magician and skeptic James (The Amazing) Randi has had a long-standing offer of 1.2 million dollars for any psychic to perform a paranormal act under controlled conditions. There have been no takers.

Exercise #5

After reading this chapter, look up the following scientifically verified supernatural occurrences on the internet or at the library.

1. The blood, sweat and tears that emerged from the statue of Mary at Akita, Japan

2. The miracle at Lanciano, Italy

3. Scientific studies done on the image of Our Lady of Guadalupe

4. Scientific studies on the Shroud of Turin (including the now resolved controversy surrounding the Carbon 14 dating challenge as explained at www.ShroudStory.com)

5. The history of Lourdes, France (www.zenit.org/english/send_friend/index.phtml?sid=57 and www.lourdes-france.org/ and then click on English flag for English)

6. The miracle of the sun at Fatima, Portugal in 1917 (www.fatima.org/library/sc01pg16.html+o+seculo+fatima+miracle&hl=en&ie=UTF-8)

7. Apparitions of Virgin Mary at Zeitun Church, Egypt (http://www.zeitun-eg.org/stmaridx.htm)

On the following pages are some descriptions of some of the supernatural occurrences listed on the last page.

There are many other miracles that have been scientifically investigated but the ones I just listed are the most prominent and irrefutable ones. But if you are fascinated by miracles and your assurance is deepened, please do continue to investigate them.

A statue of Jesus' mother, Mary, in Akita, Japan.

Scientifically verified human blood, sweat and tears pour out of a statue of Mary in Akita, Japan that X-ray machines fixed on the statue at the time of them flowing show that there is no source from within the statue that they could be coming from. And there are a number of other miracles within this miracle (mostly surrounding Sister Agnes, the nun attached to it) that can be seen by anyone who is interested in pursuing hearing this entire story.

Statue of Mary at Akita, Japan

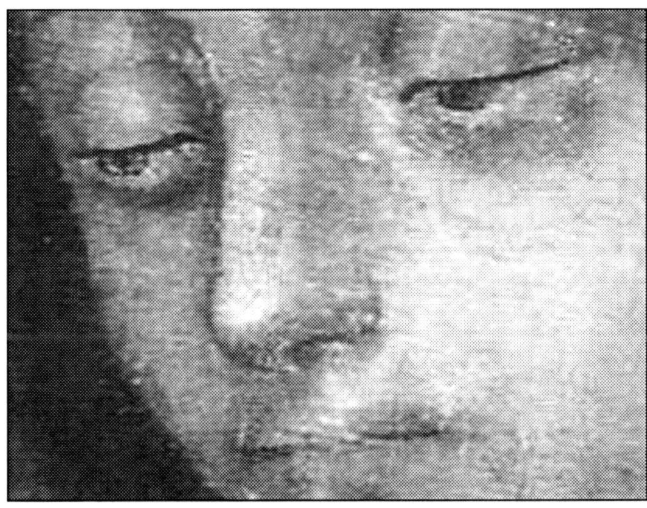

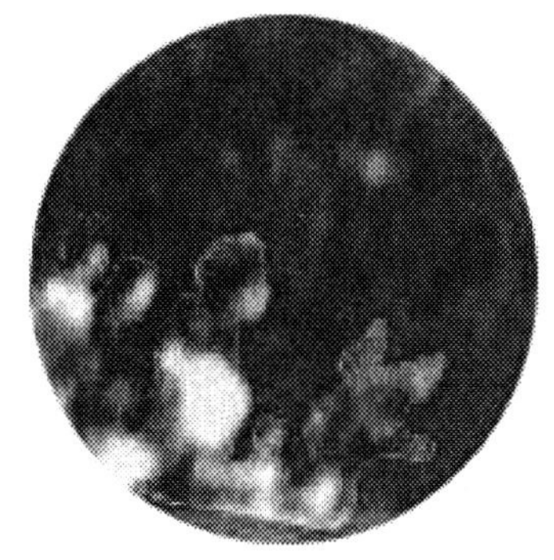

Above: Magnification of the Right Eye on Tilma of Our Lady of Guadalupe

Another example would be the eye in the cloak of our Lady of Guadalupe.

The story of Guadalupe is that, amidst terrible times between the Spanish and the Indians in Mexico in 1531, Jesus' mother, Mary, appeared to a peasant, Juan Diego, to try to give proof so that all would believe in Christianity and peace would happen between the Spanish settlers and the Indians. Towards that end she told Juan Diego that she wanted a Church to be erected at the spot where she appeared to him. The local bishop said that he needed proof to do such a huge thing. To make a long story short, Juan Diego returned to the spot where he saw Mary, where he found roses that were not supposed to be there in the winter. The roses would especially be a sign to the bishop because these were Castilian roses, indigenous to Castille, the Spanish province where the Bishop was from. Juan Diego returned to the bishop to show him the roses that he carried in his cloak. When he unfurled the cloak, not only did the roses come out, but an image of Mary appeared on

his cloak. Because of this cloak, within 10 years, an estimated 9 million Aztecs gazed at the image and were baptized Christians. This cloak still exists today.

Now let's look at what science has done to verify the supernatural nature of this.

The tilma (cloak) itself is made from the fibers of the maguey plant, which does not last more than 25-40 years. Yet after 473 years, the original tilma can still be found in perfect condition in the Basilica of Our Lady of Guadalupe on Tepeyac. Also, NASA photographic research revealed that in the eyes of the image of Mary on the cloak are scenes that include a number of people. There are some men kneeling, some are Indian and some are wearing religious clothing. Furthermore, these reflections appear in a manner and at an angle which matches precisely that of what each human eye would see.

Further research reveals even the presence of blood vessels and capillaries within the eye. No human artist could have ever painted this. Not in this detail, not on this material, and not with colors that no one has been able to duplicate since.

And if that weren't enough, French astronomers have determined that the layout of the stars on her green-blue colored mantel, match precisely what someone in Mexico would have seen in the sky in December of 1531. The arrangement of the constellations is exactly as they would have been then. Here are some excerpts that the Zenit News Agency reported in an article on January 15, 2001.

"SCIENCE STUNNED BY VIRGIN OF GUADALUPE'S EYES... Engineer Sees a Reflection, Literally, from a Scene in 1531... Rome- Digital technology is giving new leads in understanding a phenomenon that continues to puzzle science: the mysterious eyes of the image of Virgin of Guadalupe. Last week in Rome, results of research into the famed image were discussed by engineer Dr. José Aste Tonsmann at a conference at the Pontifical Athenaeum Regina Apostolorum. For over 20 years, this graduate of environmental systems engineering of Cornell University has studied the image of the Virgin left on the rough maguey fiber fabric of Juan Diego's tilma [cape] starting in 1979 while working at IBM, where he scanned at very high resolutions a very good photograph.

Though the dimensions are microscopic, the iris and the pupils of the image's eyes have imprinted on them a highly detailed picture of at least 13 people, Tonsmann said. As early as the 18th century, scientists showed that it was impossible to paint such an image in a fabric of that texture. Tonsmann pointed out that Richard Kuhn, a Nobel Prize winner in chemistry, has found that the image did not have natural, animal or mineral colorings. Given that there were no synthetic colorings in 1531, the image is inexplicable.

In 1979, Americans Philip Callahan and Jody B. Smith studied the image with infrared rays and discovered to their surprise that there was no trace of paint and that the fabric had not been treated with any kind of technique. "[How] is it possible to explain this image and its consistency in time without colors, on a fabric that has not been treated?"

Tonsmann asked. "[How] is it possible that, despite the fact there is no paint, the colors maintain their luminosity and brilliance?" Tonsmann, a Peruvian engineer, added, "Callahan and Smith showed how the image changes in color slightly according to the angle of viewing, a phenomenon that is known by the word iridescence, a technique that cannot be reproduced with human hands."

Many people have had the opportunity to inspect the eyes on the cloak closely and directly, including more than 20 physicians and ophthalmologists.

Left: In 1250 a communion host at Lanciano, Italy was miraculously transformed to scientifically-verifiable actual human flesh and remains undeteriorated to the present day.

Then there is the miracle at Lanciano.

This is just another in a number of "supernatural" occurrences where the power that was able to suspend natural laws (in order to be able to create nature itself), continues to suspend them and hint of its existence through modern day miracles.

This particular miracle had to do with a priest in Lanciano, Italy who had a hard time believing that Jesus was really present in the communion host as the Catholic Church teaches. So one morning, while saying mass, he noticed that the host and wine that he had for communion had changed into what looked like real flesh and blood.

The amazing part here is that flesh quickly hardens (Rigor Mortis) as does blood. But this flesh and blood remain intact and undeteriorated to this day, despite the fact that this occurred over 1250 years ago.

Various investigations have been conducted about this since 1574. In 1970-'71 and taken up again partly in 1981 there took place a scientific investigation by the most illustrious scientist Professor Odoardo Linoli, eminent Professor in Anatomy and Pathological Histology and in Chemistry and Clinical Microscopy. He was assisted by Professor Ruggero Bertelli of the University of Siena.

The analyses were conducted with absolute and unquestionable scientific precision and they were documented with a series of microscopic photographs.

These analyses sustained the following conclusions:

- The Flesh is real Flesh. The Blood is real Blood.
- The Flesh and the Blood belong to the human species.
- The Flesh consists of the muscular tissue of the heart.
- In the Flesh we see present in section: the myocardium, the endocardium, the vagus nerve and also the left ventricle of the heart for the large thickness of the myocardium.
- The Flesh is a "HEART" complete in its essential structure.
- The Flesh and the Blood have the same blood-type: AB (Blood-type identical to that which Professor Baima Bollone uncovered in the Holy Shroud of Turin).
- In the Blood there were found proteins in the same normal proportions (percentage-wise) as are found in the sero-proteic make-up of fresh normal blood.
- In the Blood there were also found these minerals: chlorides, phosphorus, magnesium, potassium, sodium and calcium.
- The preservation of the Flesh and of the Blood, which were left in their natural state for twelve centuries and exposed to

the action of atmospheric and biological agents, remains an extraordinary phenomenon.

In conclusion, it may be said that Science, when called upon to testify, has given a certain and thorough response as regards the authenticity of the Eucharistic Miracle of Lanciano.

And the miracles described here are just a few of the miracles that have been verified by science. There are many more that I know of, and when I start to do a search I find that there are even MANY more that I don't know of.

And keep in mind that the process of verification of miracles by the Catholic Church is a grueling one that takes many years and a lot of investigation. The Catholic Church does not easily verify miracles and does involve scientists because they know that the credibility of the Catholic Church is on the line.

(For those who wonder why it is Mary who appears in a lot of these modern day miracles and not Jesus, it may be because Jesus said that He would have a second* coming to earth which would signify the end of the world. Therefore, it may have happened this way so as not to confuse anyone that the end had begun.) *(*Hebrews 9:28).*

So now, what about these modern-day miracles that have attachment to Church realities and which have been verified by credible scientists who are living today present this dilemma for the skeptic:

How do you explain them?

When they realize that they have no good answer for this question, they then might be open to investigating the scientific and intellectual proofs (which hopefully they will now have a piqued curiosity for and will feel are worth investing time in. And those proofs can be found in my book, *Why Are We Here?*)

☐ Building Block #7

Scrutinous, leave-no-stone-unturned, n-th degree scientific and logical analyses show that God exists and the Bible is true.

> "A little bit of science averts people from God, a lot of it takes us back to Him"
> *Louis Pasteur – a founding father of science*

Exercise #6

Read the book, *Why Are We Here?* which you downloaded with this book. This book is filled with proofs and logic that shows that science and logic can lead only to the conclusions that God exists and the Bible is all true.

Like I said before, I have extensive education and training in engineering and psychology, plus I've won awards in mathematics and scored in the highest percentile in both math and English on the SAT. And because of my developed ability in analysis, I see no credible argument or proof against the existence of God or the truthfulness of the Bible.

Of course, atheists and skeptics will often try to point things out and put a believer* on the defensive (*But the purpose of my book and this workbook is to make you more of a "knower" and less of a "believer").

But when they are put on the defensive and asked to prove their side, many errors are exposed in their proofs and logic. For example, a Dr. Hovind has a $250,000 offer to anyone who can prove that evolution is true. It has gone unclaimed.

His offer reads like this at his website:
"I have a standing offer of $250,000 to anyone who can give any empirical evidence (scientific proof) for evolution. My $250,000 offer demonstrates that the hypothesis of evolution is nothing more than a religious belief."
(www.drdino.com/cse.asp?pg=250k)

⃠ Atheism Is Logically Impossible

Plus, in my book I point out how atheism is an impossible stance to take:

"There is so much going on in this universe that we can't see. Therefore, how can anyone say for certain that there is no God? And a chapter like this could never be written to support atheism because it is much easier to gather evidence that something exists than to put forth evidence that something doesn't exist.

This is because, in order to prove that something doesn't exist, your evidence would have to be total and all conclusive. Otherwise, the possibility would still be there that the something exists. Therefore, the most anti-God position a human being could logically take would be agnostic (that is: "I don't know").

So given those things (in addition to all else I've said in this writing and that can be seen in my book), isn't it strange how the mainstream has come to support the wrong side of this issue? (Actually I do explain this in my book.)

So now that I've given some of the proofs for the existence of God and the inerrancy of the Bible, let's do something fun and very helpful in transforming your life in a positive way. (This will also train you in a skill that you will find very valuable for the rest of your life).

Exercise #7

Write down how what is said in the Bible that resolves the errors that you wrote down in Exercise 4.

But first, to help you answer that, I will reprint here what is in *Why Are We Here?* about how to do a Bible study. And I've spent many joyful hours studying the Bible in the ways that I'm going to present... tapping the greatest wisdom available on how to live our lives.

How to do a Bible study

1. First you start with a question that you want to get answered, e.g. how does God feel about divorce?

2. Next you look in a concordance to show you every place in the Bible where your key word (divorce) is mentioned. (If you don't have a concordance you can find one online for online searches as well as online Bibles with search functions.)

3. Then read all of these verses (and surrounding verses), and formulate a hypothesis that wouldn't be in disagreement with any of them, e.g. 'God hates divorce, but will allow it if there's been infidelity, or if an unbelieving spouse leaves'.

4. Now, pick some key words that relate to this topic, e.g. marriage. Look in the concordance to find every place in the Bible where your relative words are mentioned. Read all of them. But, while doing so, keep in mind your hypothesis, checking to see if any disagreements come up that might cause you to have to alter it.

After doing this, you should have a pretty solid idea of what the Bible has to say about the question you've posed. But, if there is still some confusion or controversy, there are many other tools that can help you.

There are topical books, in which the Bible's contents are categorized by topic; there are commentaries by scholars and organizations who you trust (but be careful not to take these as your only source of absolute fact); there's the Holy Spirit within you (whereby wisdom can be accessed in focused states of prayer); there's your mind's ability to logically analyze and discern; there's your ability to observe what's truly occurring in life; there are Bibles with footnotes by organizations and people you trust; you can read the entire passages around the verses you are studying; you can study and understand the full books that contain the verses you are studying (e.g. who wrote them, to whom, and why, in what setting, under what circumstances, etc.); and last but not least, you can study the texts of the Bible in the original languages they were written in through dictionaries which show you the meaning of the original language.

The original writings of the Bible were in Hebrew, Aramaic, and Greek. Therefore, any serious student of the Bible, or

any person who is dubious about accepting what the Bible says by hearing it from another person, needs to go directly to the older Hebrew and Greek manuscripts. These are also available as computer software.

There are two ways to do this kind of a study: surface and in-depth. A surface study only requires a Greek or Hebrew Interlinear Bible, and a dictionary of the language you're studying. But an in-depth study requires that you master the grammar of the language, as well as know the idioms of the language of the times that the texts were written. Also, you'd have to know the customs of the day to fully grasp the meaning behind the idioms.

But, how much of all of this is really necessary? Just until you get to the point where you're sure that your hypothesis finds no contradiction from any of the above tests (and to the depths of your heart-of-hearts you know that you're not fooling yourself)."

So back to the question: **How does what is said in the Bible resolve the errors you listed in Exercise 4?**

____

____

____

____

____

____

Evidence for the validity of the Bible:

My being convinced about the Bible was solidified by my many years of experience with it, based on:

(1) I tested its precepts and finding them to only lead to good, both in my life and my inner experience...including the fact that it felt really good.

(2) I found no errors in the Bible that couldn't be resolved

(3) I found only positive and exciting revelations about the real life that I live in and can observe, that led to greater understandings and clearer seeing that resonated throughout my entire being.

(4) The solutions presented in the Bible greatly improved my life and gave practical, effective ways to resolve all of my problems.

(5) I've had tremendous experiences in Christianity and in prayer that can only be reported and attempted to be described, but cannot be fully transmitted to another (although I can encourage others to do the same things that I did that made me receptive to these experiences which is prayer). I can say they have been the peak experiences of my life.

(6) For the first time, and after much searching, I could observe within me that my "restless heart" was restless no more. That alone was worth the price of admission.

(7) After all of what I just said, I don't see how life can be effectively and fully lived with deep fulfillment and great purpose without the Bible and a heart relationship with God.

And of course, as a testimony to the effectiveness of the Bible what could be added to all of this from other sources:

1. American history shows a proportionate decline in the social statistics (such as more crime, higher divorce rate, etc.) as the Bible became less and less revered and followed in America.

2. The effectiveness of actually following the Bible...which can be proven on the society level (for example, by the stories of Shimabuku, Japan and the Welsh Revival) and on the personal level (by my testimony and the testimonies of many others).

3. The many proofs that I present in my book from many different scientific and logical viewpoints.

(1) The fact that the Bible says that this Creation-that-wasn't-made-by-humans alone will be reason enough for God to hold us accountable for His existence, and the fact the He wrote His laws on our heart will alone be reason enough for us to be accountable whether our behavior was good or bad on earth.

(2) The fact that the Scientific Method yields a proof of God and the 100% credibility of the Bible (which can be seen in my book).

(3) No one has a logically legitimate right to criticize the Bible unless they've read it and tried on its precepts.

(4) There are no counter-arguments that are provable.

Workbook Review:

■ Building Block #1

What Jesus and the Bible say proved to be the most intellectually sound and effective when applied.

■ Building Block #2

Being that we have to choose a personal approach to life, I found (after my MANY experiences, involvements and studies) that the greatest choice possible in the world as to what to pattern my life after is the Bible. But that means every word in the Bible and a correct overall and specific understanding of what they mean.

■ Building Block #3

Being that we are creatures with needs outside of ourselves, and being that those things require involvement with other people, we have to align with something more than ourselves. I found that the most advanced system in the world is in the Bible.

■ Building Block #4

Jesus and the Bible are the greatest source of psychological and sociological solutions in human history.

Building Block #5

It is not logical or historical to think that Jesus' miracles and resurrection didn't occur.

Building Block #6

If you want scientifically proven modern day miracles... these also exist and have been proven by scientists and can be verified by your senses in the present.

Building Block #7

A scrutinizing, leave-no-stone-unturned, nth degree scientific and logical analysis shows that God exists and the Bible is true.

Continuing Your Journey

Now that you have scientific and logical proof that God exists and the Bible is true you will undoubtedly want to study the Bible and find truths for your life. You might first want to learn more about what God really is like.

Here is an additional exercise to ponder:

What is God really like? (compared to what I feel or unconsciously think he is like?)

If you believe God exists, what is God like for you emotionally? For example, does God feel distant, close, always there, never there, sometimes there/sometimes not available, kind, angry, ready to pounce on you, has impossible of standards, strict, permissive, can never be pleased with you, or is happy with you no matter what you do, etc. etc.?? Write down your answer below.

Now answer the same question as the previous one, but this time write down how you felt and feel emotionally about your own father, mother, and other authority figures in your life as a child. For example, was your father always there, never there, close, distant, kind, strict, permissive, etc.

Was there any similarity between your feelings toward God and your parents as far as how you think or feel about them and in what ways?

The reason for the last question is that there is sometimes a tendency to have unconscious ideas about God from how we view or feel about our parents, kind of like projecting what we experience from our parents onto our concept of God...

Take a look inside to see if this factors into your concepts of God at all and how this dynamic might affect your feelings or thoughts about God now. If they are, in what way?

Of course the real God is not the same as our limited ideas of God or how we view or feel about our parents, even though our parents are in a sense a symbol of God for us as a child.

Just a little psychological insight is that some people when they read the Bible even seem to zero in on the traits that they believe God is like and don't notice or really let other traits register with them (like we tend to see what we already feel or believe) so if we want to know what the God of the Bible is really like we need to consciously and meticulously read what it says... especially what Jesus said in the New Testament... to get a true idea of what the Bible is saying about God.

So in reading the Bible, especially the New Testament, keep an eye open for finding God's real traits and keep a record here:

For example, God is: merciful, gracious, slow to anger and kind *(Exod. 34:6)* and love *(1John 4:16)*

Write down some things about what God is really like from the Bible:

____

____

____

____

____

Benefits

If a person wants to receive the benefits that I list for *Why Are We Here?* they need to make total obedience to the Bible the #1 goal and priority in their life. The way that my book gives them the ability to do that is that it gives them the rock foundation that Jesus talked about (or the brick house of the 3rd pig in the children's story, The 3 Little Pigs), clearing all mental doubt and giving them the understanding as to why they should make total obedience to the Bible their #1 priority.

The #1 Goal In Life

If you lived in communist China and knew for absolute sure that if you held a public rally against the government that you would be tortured to death immediately and no one would know, you wouldn't do it. Why? Not only because of basic survival instincts, but because you would be more valuable to your cause and message if you remained alive. Well, in order to be able to have the internal benefits that

I've described that a person will get if they read, understand and apply what is in *Why Are We Here?*, it is all dependent on them making obedience to God as he teaches us in the Bible and through His Spirit, the top priority in their life. That, I have found, is the only thing that works in being able to create those benefits. And I first tried nearly everything else.

I mean, a lot of people believe in the Bible and can even quote Scripture. BUT...do they obey it above all else? (Jesus said that even satan can quote Scripture and that some who call Him Lord and have done works in His name will not go to Heaven.) That is, do they have the same fear to disobey it that the person in the China example has to disobey the Chinese government? The Bible says that wisdom begins with the fear of the Lord. You might be thinking "But I thought we were supposed to love God and that He loves us too". That's true. But we don't fear Him...we fear what His just responses must be to sin. That is, when we're holy, great feelings come through us...but when we aren't, then unpleasant experiences must come through us to help guide us to get back on a holy track. That is what is necessary to try to maintain a system of good. So a person who wants a system of good should be able to respect that.

So that all leads to a basic rock solid realization: If we want to align with good, and we don't want to incur the unpleasant repercussions that automatically have to come with bad...we simply never do what is bad and always do what is good. *Then* we have to be *absolutely* convinced that the Bible, without error, is the one place in the world that defines what is good and what is bad. Without that absolute

knowledge we might choose to yield to some of the pressures from within us and outside of us...even if those pressures lead to actions that go against what the Bible says.

This is why *Why Are We Here?* focuses so much on the "basics" (the existence of God and the fact that the Bible is all true). Without knowing those things, there won't be the fortitude to not yield to pressures, especially while living in this world that so much goes against what the Bible says, and even glorifies evil. Therefore *Why Are We Here?* turns over every stone so as to remove all doubt about the "basics". Also, there is a "lab" part to this experiment, and that is to see how following or not following the Bible in our real lives affects us. That's why applying what the Bible says to do and not do is also critical. By doing that, we can gain an appreciation for the Bible's superiority as *the* guide for our life...which will further increase our trust in it. Also, keep in mind that another essential skill here is a constant awareness of the feedback from the Holy Spirit, because it is the Holy Spirit who shows us what Scripture means... above our own thinking and others' interpretations.

Here is what our order of priorities should be for 'who and what to listen to and follow' (from top to bottom).

The Bible/Holy Spirit
Our needs
Our feelings
Our thoughts
Other people/groups
Things we read and hear

And the bottom five all have to be funneled through the top one to see if they are okay.

Let's look at how this priority might fail to happen in a person's life.

Under "Other people/groups" can even be included religious people. Early on I was given some bad advice by a church person that was based on a misinterpretation of Scripture. Therefore, although in some instances you can start perhaps with the thoughts of the most trusted religious sources you know, you must filter those thoughts through the Bible and Holy Spirit. Therefore, the most important skill that a person needs to develop is their own independent, personal relationship with the Bible and the Holy Spirit.

If you blindly rely solely on people (all of whom the Bible says are imperfect to a degree) then you will be risking incorporating error into your foundation. But if you rely on God (who is perfect) then you will have ensured for yourself

a safeguard against error. The Bible verse that shows us how to approach this is 1John 2:27: "*As for you, the anointing that you received from him remains in you, so that you do not need anyone to teach you. But his anointing teaches you about everything and is true and not false.*" And by "anointing" it means that Jesus left us with a "helper" ... the Holy Spirit. As far as not needing a teacher, it doesn't mean that we don't expose ourselves to teaching. No, it is perfectly fine and helpful to expose ourselves to teachers. But all of what they say is processed through the Holy Spirit as to whether what we are hearing or reading is true or not. But that only works for a person who is clearly in touch with the Holy Spirit and has isolated and amplified His voice within (as opposed to the voices that come from the mind, subconscious mind, emotional heart, body, others and the world). I have taught the technique on how to do that in *Why Are We Here?*.

And keep in mind that the Bible says that the Holy Spirit speaks in a "spiritual", not verbal, language. 1Cor. 2:12-15: *"We have not received the spirit of the world but the Spirit that is from God, so that we may understand the things freely given us by God. And we speak about them not with words taught by human wisdom, but with words taught by the Spirit, describing spiritual realities in spiritual terms. Now the natural person does not accept what pertains to the Spirit of God, for to him it is foolishness, and he cannot understand it, because it is judged spiritually. The spiritual person, however, can judge everything but is not subject to judgment by anyone."*

And know that there are many in the world who claim to be saying things that the Holy Spirit gave them. But the Holy

Spirit in you will show you (always via a spiritual impression and sometimes with reasoning that will manifest in your mind) if what they are saying is true or not (assuming that you've developed the ability to clearly hear Him). But a *feeling* of truth must be there. Hearing the Holy Spirit is one of the two most important skills in life, so treat developing it with that much importance.

The second most important skill says that being a Bible scholar should be the highest interest of a person's mind. You might be thinking, "Why isn't basic survival and needs in the highest spot?" That is because: the Bible is where we find out how to best approach basic survival and needs. In fact those are the areas where the world errs the most, which makes the Bible all the more valuable and needed.

Therefore I can't emphasize enough the fact that *complete* confidence in, fear of and obedience to the Bible (in conjunction with a very strong and clear hearing of the Holy Spirit. John 16:13: "The Spirit of truth will guide you to all truth." has to be absolute in order for the great emotional benefits (and lack of unpleasant corrections) that God has to offer to take place.

Here are some of the benefits that come from making the Bible your #1 source of guidance and how they happen:

- You will be INSPIRED when you see the great purpose in every moment of your life
- You will NEVER FEEL INTIMIDATED AGAIN by any thought from others or the world
- You will be CONFIDENT that you will know how to handle in the best way possible any confusion or problem that might arise
- You will feel ASSURED, PEACEFUL and even EXCITED about death and what happens afterwards
- You will experience the SECURITY of having a perfect internal and external guide for the BEST LIFE POSSIBLE now
- You will NEVER BE BORED again
- You will experience DEEP FULFILLMENT and INNER PEACE
- You will gain POWER over any negative inclinations or impulses
- You will have a great SELF-ESTEEM
- You will learn how to find rest in the ULTIMATE OASIS in this world
- You will be THANKFUL IN ALL CIRCUMSTANCES
- You will see how to consider life all JOY
- You will NEVER BE ANXIOUS about money
- You will NEVER WORRY

Take the following Faith Test to see where you stand. The Bible tells us that we can experience what is stated above. As a Bible study exercise, you could jot down the verses that apply to each of the questions below. (Chapter 2 of *Why Are We Here?* shows you how to do a Bible study.) If you aren't experiencing these goods things your life yet, take time to memorize the verses and pray about these things asking God for all you need as Jesus said to: *"Ask and you shall receive"* and *"Seek and you will find."*

1. Are you always inspired?

____

____

____

____

____

____

2. Do you have a deep inner peace?

____

____

____

____

____

____

3. Are you never intimidated by family, friends, co-workers, strangers, authorities, media, or the world in general?

4. Do you always have a feeling of confidence?

5. Do you have power to not give into impulses to sin?

6. Can you easily handle decisions?

7. Are you never confused about life?

8. Are you deeply fulfilled?

9. Do you have great inspirations in your life?

10. Are you confident that you understand this life?

11. Do you feel assured about what happens after you die?

12. Are you confident that God exists?

13. Are you sure that the Bible is completely true?

14. Are you never bored?

15. Do you have good self-esteem?

16. Are you confident that your prayers are heard?

17. Do you feel sure about what you're doing with your life?

18. Do you feel good about where your life is heading?

19. Do you know where to find answers to questions about life?

20. Do you never worry about anything including money?

21. Are you thankful in all circumstances?

____

____

____

____

____

____

____

22. Do you consider your life all joy?

____

____

____

____

____

____

____

Thank you

for taking time to go through this workbook.
(We thank you and God is pleased that you are taking the time to get to know Him better.)

We encourage you to continue in your study and search for even more of *the* truth.

Product Catalog

(1) Why Are We Here? $14.50
Includes the proven meaning of life is in such a way that the reader really understands it. It's an essential companion for this workbook.

(2) Addiction Free Forever $19.95
How to permanently and naturally cure an alcohol or drug addiction.

(3) Addiction Free Forever Workbook $19.95
This workbook allows you to take a full inventory of your life and experience and in 10 steps takes you through a transformation to being addiction free.

(4) Sweeping It Under The Drug..$14.95
This book takes an overall look at what addiction is and talks about all the various forms.

(5) Personal Coaching (phone or email) ....$35/half hour

Plus more including downloadable products can be purchased at:
www.UltimateTruths.com
www.AddictionFreeForever.com/orders.html

Or you can order any of these items by mail by photocopying this page (or hand write or type what you want). Include your name, address and phone. Send a check or money order for the total, plus shipping and handling, to:

Lighthouse Publishing
PO Box 40
Gladstone, OR 97027 USA

Shipping & Handling Inside USA:
Order Total 0-$19.99 = $3.50 S&H; $20-49.99 = $4.75;
$50-99.99 = $5.50 (Canadian Orders: Add $2.00 to above.)

Some Reviews and Quotes for *Why Are We Here?* by Dennis Marcellino

"This is a very important book that is greatly needed at this time. I agree that the Bible should be the ultimate resource for life and living and that the world could greatly benefit from being logically and scientifically shown that this is true."
Mark Victor Hansen, Co-author, New York Times #1 Best-Selling "Chicken Soup For The Soul" series

"*Why are We Here?* is a book for everyone. Have you ever wondered what Christians actually believe? Now, you can find out without having to ask anyone. Dennis Marcellino has written a well organized account of why we are here. Marcellino, who has a wide range of education, has written an organized account with out being overly scientific or overly pushy with his personal beliefs. Interestingly enough, it is his musical abilities that you would most likely know him for, having belonged to the Tokens who had the hit, "The Lion Sleeps Tonight." I highly recommend "*WHY WE ARE HERE?*" to Christians and "Non-Christians" alike will gain information here. Christians will have an organized account of what they believe and why. Others will have an account of what Christians believe and why.
Deven Vasko of Betsie's Literary Page

"Dennis Marcellino is clearly an authority on the scientific evidence that proves that God exists... a prerequisite to knowing WHY WE ARE HERE! And unlike others who give proofs, which are often difficult-to-grasp, micro-science proofs, his are simple and easy to understand. (Not having this information is like) getting on a horse and riding in all directions. If you want to settle the questions that when answered will bring true peace of mind and abundance, then I highly recommend you tune out the rest of the world and tune into what this fascinating expert has to share. "
Randy Gilbert, Bestselling author of "Success Bound"

"Why Are We Here? is the scientific answer to an age-old question and readers don't need to be a scientist or philosopher to understand. It was written with the intent of investigating what could be scientifically concluded about theology and its related fields. *Why Are We Here?* is engaging reading and a highly recommended addition to any philosophy and theological reading list surveying the general questions related to the meaning of life."
James A. Cox, Internet Bookwatch

"Dennis Marcellino has the answer. Actually, with an education that ranges from science and engineering to theology and psychology, Marcellino has many answers. But in his new book, *Why Are We Here?*, he chooses to answer the one question that has puzzled intellectuals for centuries."
Laura Gunderson, Clackamas Review

"You get an awful lot of research, thought, work and wisdom condensed into this one book. It's not a sloppy nor sentimental work but a rigorous and joyous proof... All this for $14.50...that's hard to beat!"
Dave Kirby, Book Bit, WTBF-FM, Troy, Alabama

"I highly recommend *Why Are We Here?* as a must book for anyone's library."
Tony Trupiano, Talk Show Host, Talk America Radio Network

"*Why Are We Here?* was a fun book and very easy to read. It was very enjoyable and a great read for me."
Nancy London, host, WXCI-FM, Western Connecticut State University

"Dennis Marcellino is such a prolific writer and thinker."
Susan Filkins, Rose Sparrows Literary Agency, New York

"*Why Are We Here?* should be rated one of the best in Apologetics. I could hardly put it down."
Nate Camacho, seminarian at Calvary Chapel School of Ministry

"A wonderful book! The author marries his science/engineering background with his cultural/musician experiences. This book is an A to Z about life... a sequential journey starting with the origins issue, all the way through to the end of life and beyond. You should buy 10 copies and give them to your family, friends, people in your church and co-workers!"
Steve Carr, Talk Show Host for "Destiny", WYLL, Chicago

"This book really does answer the question 'What is the meaning of life?' in a very logically satisfying and inspiring way. And it is also filled with fresh, insightful reflections on all aspects of life that uplift and enlighten the reader... *Why Are We Here?* gives an excellent overview of life while scientifically determining what is true and what isn't true among the doctrinal differences between the Christian denominations, world religions, psychology approaches, new age and secular philosophies. He has done a fantastic job in putting together this extremely valuable book. Obviously I highly, highly recommend it!"
Mark Stefani, Vision Reviews

"In using science to explore what is usually an emotionally charged subject, Marcellino provides a strong fact-based philosophical approach which is compelling."
Diane Donovan, The Philosopher's Bookshelf, Midwest Book Review

"*Why Are We Here?* answered all my questions, and is written in a very informative, "down to earth," manner. It is wonderful! It is one of the most helpful books I've ever read. I Love It!
Ann, Ohio

"Dennis has a very interesting...a VERY interesting story to tell!"
Joe Galuski, WSYR, Syracuse, NY

"The greatest book ever! If people would just read it and really look at what it's saying! He explains it scientifically, and there's no way that anybody can dispute it. He's a genius."
Jerry, Vancouver, WA

Printed in the United States
80417LV00005B/1-50

9 780945 272120